Think Like a Scientist

THE HISTORY OF THE SCIENTIFIC METHOD

Heather Moore Niver

Britannica
Educational Publishing
IN ASSOCIATION WITH
ROSEN
EDUCATIONAL SERVICES

Published in 2019 by Britannica Educational Publishing (a trademark of Encyclopædia Britannica, Inc.) in association with The Rosen Publishing Group, Inc.
29 East 21st Street, New York, NY 10010

Distributed exclusively by Rosen Publishing.
To see additional Britannica Educational Publishing titles, go to rosenpublishing.com.

First Edition

Britannica Educational Publishing
J.E. Luebering: Executive Director, Core Editorial
Mary Rose McCudden: Editor, Britannica Student Encyclopedia

Rosen Publishing
Amelie von Zumbusch: Editor
Nelson Sá: Art Director
Brian Garvey: Series Designer
Tahara Anderson: Book Layout
Cindy Reiman: Photography Manager
Karen Huang: Photo Researcher

Library of Congress Cataloging-in-Publication Data

Names: Niver, Heather Moore, author.
Title: The history of the scientific method / Heather Moore Niver.
Description: New York : Britannica Educational Publishing, in Association with Rosen Educational Services, 2019. | Series: Think like a scientist | Audience: Grades 3–6. | Includes bibliographical references and index.
Identifiers: LCCN 2017055973| ISBN 9781538302309 (library bound) | ISBN 9781538302316 (pbk.) | ISBN 9781538302323 (6 pack)
Subjects: LCSH: Science—Methodology—History—Juvenile literature. | Observation (Scientific method)—History—Juvenile literature.
Classification: LCC Q175.2 .N58 2019 | DDC 507.2—dc23
LC record available at https://lccn.loc.gov/2017055973

Manufactured in the United States of America

Photo credits: Cover, p. 1 Apic/Hulton Archive/Getty Images; cover (top), back cover, interior pages background cetus/Shutterstock.com; p. 5 © Encyclopædia Britannica, Inc; p. 7 Marie-Lan Nguyen; p. 8 © Courtesy of the National Library of Medicine (Image ID: 192922); p. 9 Science History Images/Alamy Stock Photo; pp. 10, 11, 17 Photos.com/Thinkstock; pp. 12, 20 © National Library of Medicine, Bethesda, Md.; p. 13 Universal Images Group/Getty Images; p. 15 © Statens Museum for Kunst (National Gallery of Denmark); www.smk.dk (Public domain); p. 19 © Courtesy of the National Portrait Gallery, London; p. 21 © Archiv für Kunst und Geschichte, Berlin; p. 22 Yale Center for British Art, Paul Mellon Collection, B1977.14.13111.; pp. 24, 25 Sueddeutsche Zeitung Photo/Alamy Stock Photo; p. 26 blickwinkel/Alamy Stock Photo; p. 27 FatCamera/E+/Getty Images.

CONTENTS

CHAPTER 1

Introducing the Scientific Method

Scientists solve problems using the scientific method. It's a step-by-step process that all scientists try to follow.

Scientists start by finding out as much as possible about a problem. Then they make a hypothesis. They test the hypothesis with an experiment. Then they analyze the results, or the data, to see if the hypothesis was right. If the experiment does not support the hypothesis, they think about the problem again and develop a new hypothesis. They then test that hypothesis with a new experiment. If the experiment supports the hypothesis, other scientists repeat the experiment to make sure that they get the same results. If they do get the same

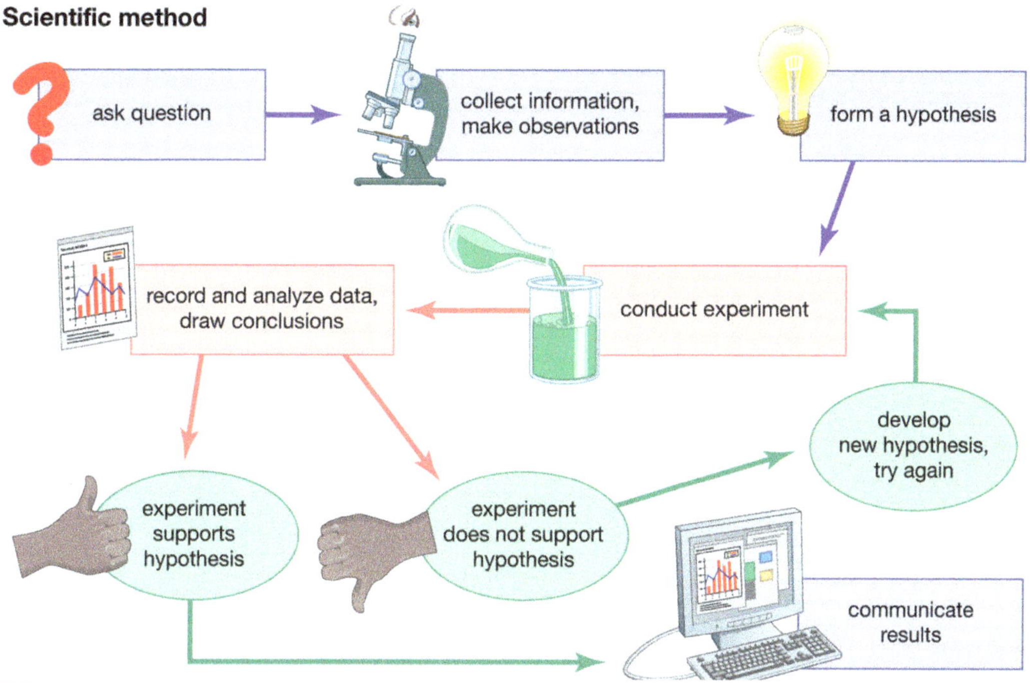

The scientific method is the process scientists follow to solve problems. Scientists conduct experiments and carefully record, analyze, and evaluate the data.

results, the hypothesis is accepted as true until it can be proven false.

Scientists use the information they learn from testing many hypotheses to develop **scientific theories**. A theory

VOCABULARY

Scientific theories are explanations for why things work or how things happen.

COMPARE & CONTRAST

Scientific laws sum up a wide range of observations and results of experiments. Scientific theories are explanations for observations and results. Can you think of a scientific theory and a scientific law? How do they compare?

is a much broader explanation than a hypothesis. Scientists consider theories to be the best explanations for why some things happen in the natural world. A theory may later need to be changed if scientists discover new information about the subject.

Historians trace the roots of the scientific method to the ancient Greeks. **Philosophers** like Plato felt that reasoning was the way

VOCABULARY

Philosophers are people who seek wisdom or enlightenment, such as scholars or thinkers.

to all knowledge. Plato's student Aristotle believed that people could learn everything about the world using logic. He argued that any theory must be based on observed facts.

The doctor Hippocrates made detailed observations of his patients and thought that diseases had a physical cause. Before that, people believed that diseases were caused by the gods or evil spirits.

Aristotle thought that people could learn anything they wanted if they put logic to use.

Another influence was Galen of Pergamum. He kept detailed notes about his treatment of injured gladiators. The notes show a methodical technique for treating and curing wounds and illnesses.

Philosophers from the ancient Arab world added to the work of the ancient Greeks. Almost a thousand years ago Ibn al-Haytham created a method based on careful measuring and experimenting. It is like the scientific method used by modern scientists.

Galen of Pergamum took incredibly detailed notes about how he treated injured gladiators.

Ibn al-Haytham studied the world around him carefully. If he noticed a problem or something that he did not understand, he would come up with an idea to explain what he saw. His explanation was based on study and experiments. In order to test his idea he would perform more experiments. He then studied the results and came to a conclusion. Once he was able to explain the problem, he shared the explanation with others by publishing the results.

Other Arab scientists built on his work. For example, Al-Rahwi was the first to argue that multiple experiments should be conducted before a conclusion could be determined. Jabir ibn Hayyan, introduced the concept of **controlled experiments**.

If Ibn al-Haytham didn't understand something, he experimented to figure out an explanation.

VOCABULARY

In **controlled experiments**, a scientist keeps all the parts the same except one, called a variable. Changing the variable allows the scientist to compare different results.

CHAPTER 2

THE SCIENTIFIC METHOD DEVELOPS

The work of Arab scientists and thinkers influenced people in Europe during the Middle Ages. One of these was a man named Roger Bacon, who lived in England in the 1200s. Bacon also felt that true science should be based on observation and experiment.

According to Roger Bacon, observation and experiment are the basis for true science.

During a period we call the Renaissance, humans made big discoveries in many different areas. This included science. In Europe at that time (in the sixteenth and seventeenth centuries), advances in science were so important that we now call it a scientific revolution. One important scientist was Nicolaus Copernicus. He was an astronomer—a scientist who studies the movements of planets and stars. As a result of his studies Copernicus said that Earth moves around the sun. Before that, most people thought the sun revolved around Earth.

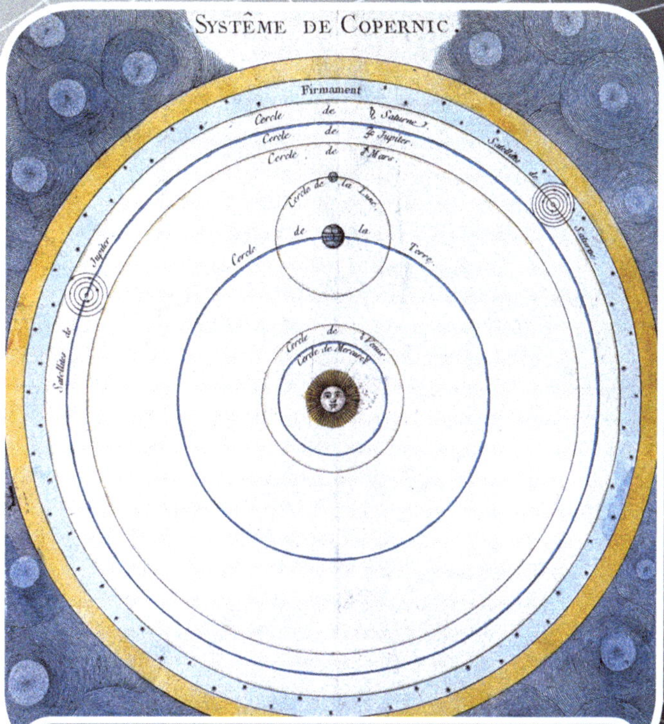

This illustration shows Nicolaus Copernicus's revolutionary idea: that Earth and other planets travel around the sun.

THINK ABOUT IT

In the Middle Ages, scholars usually got their scientific knowledge from books. During the Renaissance, people began to experiment and observe for themselves. What do you think inspired people to start thinking differently?

Flemish physician and surgeon Andreas Vesalius performed careful dissections of cadavers, or dead bodies. He thought that by looking inside human bodies as a scientist, he would learn more about them than just looking at the outside.

This woodcut, probably by Andreas Vesalius himself, is from his *Seven Books on the Structure of the Human Body*.

He made drawings from his observations. They were published in 1543 in his *Seven Books on the Structure of the Human Body.*

Around the same time, in the 1500s, Galileo Galilei made a special telescope to look at the sky. He observed carefully and collected lots of data. Galileo discovered four moons circling the planet Jupiter. This helped to provide evidence supporting Copernicus's theory that Earth revolves around the sun. Galileo made many discoveries in a lot of different areas. These

An illustration shows Galileo demonstrating his telescope to the doge Leonardo Dona.

included his theories of motion. Thanks to his work, experiments became a common method for discovering how nature works.

Francis Bacon contributed to the scientific revolution of the seventeenth century. He carefully studied the works of Copernicus and Galileo. Bacon was the first to create a formal scientific method. He thought that all discoveries in science should be the result of a three-stage process: observation, experimentation, and analysis and inductive reasoning. He believed that the human race depended on an

COMPARE & CONTRAST

Using either a general principle or specific data to draw a specific conclusion is deductive reasoning. Using established facts to draw a general conclusion is inductive reasoning. This is the kind of logic normally used in the sciences. These kinds of reasoning are considered opposites. How are they alike?

understandable method of scientific questioning.

The French philosopher René Descartes thought of the universe as a gigantic machine. He thought that anyone who understood the fundamental rules of the universe would also be able to figure out how anything will act. He insisted that knowledge in the sciences should be based not on probabilities but on certainties derived from observations and experiments.

This oil painting of the French philosopher René Descartes by Frans Hals is dated about 1649. Descartes famously wrote, "I think, therefore I am."

CHAPTER 3

Standing on the Shoulders of Giants

THINK ABOUT IT

In the peer review process, experts in a field help judge the value of a work or idea. These judges cannot be part of the work they are judging. Why do you think having independent judges is important?

In 1660, scientists in London, England, organized the Royal Society to oversee the sharing of information. The society felt that evidence from experiments was more important than theoretical evidence. This was a great step for the scientific method. The expert panel and a journal (for publishing information) also created a peer review process.

In 1703 English scientist Isaac Newton was elected president of the Royal Society. Newton argued that the scientific method required both deductive and inductive reasoning. He established some basic rules for scientists to follow using the scientific method. These rules are thought

Isaac Newton is responsible for some of the fundamental rules behind the modern scientific method.

of as better than the rules of scientists who came before him.

Newton's work marks the beginning of modern science. Although Newton is revered for his brilliant ideas, he said, "If I have seen further it is only by standing on the shoulders of giants."

Bacon's and Newton's ideas about the scientific method continued to be the primary approach for the next three hundred years. Eventually natural philosophy (as science was known until the nineteenth century) broke up into different areas, such as chemistry, physics, and biology. However, many scientists in these more specific areas continued to advance the scientific method through experimentation.

The Irish scientist Robert Boyle is known as the "father of chemistry." Boyle's scientific work is characterized by its reliance on experiment and observation. He was reluctant to formulate generalized theories. In 1665 he defined "necessary repeatability," in which he determined that in order for an experiment's results to be considered valid, they must be repeated.

Frenchman Antoine-Laurent Lavoisier is known for his controlled, precise chemistry experiments. By brilliant experiments and exact measurements, Lavoisier proved that burning, the rusting of metals, and the breathing of animals all had something in common. They all consisted

Robert Boyle has become known as the "father of chemistry," thanks to his work based on experiments and observation.

Antoine-Laurent Lavoisier is famous for having proven that the processes of substances burning, metals rusting, and animals breathing are connected.

of the union of oxygen with other chemicals. Since this union, called oxidation, is one of the most important chemical processes, his discovery started the development of modern chemistry.

In the eighteenth century, a British doctor named James Lind saw that more soldiers died of a disease called scurvy than of wounds from combat. So he compared the effects of citrus fruits on patients with scurvy against five alternative remedies. He showed that the fruit was noticeably better than vinegar, cider, seawater, and other remedies. In doing so, Lind determined the cause of scurvy. He also

THINK ABOUT IT

A clinical trial is formal testing of a specific treatment. New drugs or other treatments go through testing and studies to see if they have better health benefits, safety, or cost. How do you think the scientific method relates to this kind of testing?

James Lind realized too many soldiers were dying of scurvy. He used a type of clinical trial to find the cure.

Edward Jenner conducted multiple experiments to prove his controversial hypothesis that infecting people with cowpox would protect them from getting smallpox.

used an early version of a clinical trial.

The English physician Edward Jenner created a vaccine for smallpox, the leading cause of death at the time. In May 1796, Jenner used a less harmful substance called cowpox to inoculate a boy against smallpox. His hypothesis was that by infecting someone with cowpox, that person would be protected from smallpox. The boy became slightly sick but was well after ten days. On July 1, Jenner inoculated the boy a second time. This time he used smallpox matter. No disease developed; protection was complete. His experiments included observation, hypothesis, testing, and a conclusion. Jenner repeated his experiments a few times to prove his hypothesis was correct.

CHAPTER 4

The Scientific Method in Modern Times

During the twentieth century, several philosophers contributed to the scientific method. Karl Popper insisted that hypotheses must be testable. Popper also argued that the best test for a scientific hypothesis is one that tries to disprove it, not prove it. If the hypothesis cannot be disproven, then it is true.

Karl Popper argued that failing to disprove a hypothesis is the best test to prove that it is true.

Thomas Kuhn believed that scientific progress depended on shifts in paradigms, or scientific worldviews. He argued that the paradigm determines the kinds of experiments scientists perform, the types of questions they ask, and the problems they consider important

Paul Feyerabend believed that it was foolish for different **disciplines** to follow a single set of rules. He pointed out that many amazing discoveries, such as those of Galileo and Copernicus,

Paul Feyerabend reasoned that no scientist should be bound to any one set of rules, not even the scientific method.

VOCABULARY

Disciplines are branches of science.

These epidemiologists test dead birds to study the causes of bird flu.

would not have been made if they had limited themselves to the rules of the scientific method.

Still, many modern scientists use the scientific method today. By learning what causes a disease, scientists can work to control its spread. Imagine there was a terrible disease outbreak, and people were becoming ill and dying. An **epidemiologist** might use the scientific method to question, observe, analyze, test and experiment, and conclude what is causing the illness and deaths.

VOCABULARY

An **epidemiologist** is a person who specializes in epidemiology, or the study of how diseases spread.

Anyone can use the scientific method to solve basic questions or problems. For example, what happens to seed

The scientific method can be used to find out how seeds grow under different types of light bulbs.

growth if you use light bulbs with different levels of brightness?

- **Question:** What problem needs solving? What do you want to learn—perhaps if different light bulbs affect seed growth?
- **Research:** Look up useful information in places such as the internet or books.
- **Hypothesis:** Form an educated guess about what you think will solve your problem. Maybe seeds will grow faster under brighter lights.
- **Experiment:** Create a test to learn whether or not your hypothesis is correct. Plant several different pots with grass seed. Place each pot under a light of different brightness, or wattage.
- **Analysis:** Record the results of your experiment. Write down what happens in each pot of seeds every day for four weeks, for example.

This information is called data.

- **Conclusion:** Review all data. Was your hypothesis correct? Did the seeds under the brightest light grow faster than the others?

People still talk about the scientific method today. Some still disagree on the best way to implement it. But without it, we would not know as much as we do today!

THINK ABOUT IT

Not every scientist thinks the scientific method is the perfect way to do research. Why do you think this might be true? Can you think of any cases when the scientific method would not be useful?

GLOSSARY

cowpox A disease in cows that is caused by a virus and, when passed on to human beings, produces a rash and protects against smallpox.

data Facts about something that can be used in calculating, reasoning, or planning.

deductive reasoning Reasoning in which the conclusion follows necessarily from a general rule or principle.

epidemiology A branch of science that deals with disease.

gladiators People engaged in fights to the death for public entertainment in ancient Rome.

hypothesis An attempt to explain a problem.

inductive reasoning Reasoning relating to, using, or based on induction.

logic Careful reasoning.

methodical In a careful, well-thought-out way.

Middle Ages A period of European history lasting from about the years 500 to 1500.

oxidation The process of oxidizing, or removing hydrogen from something, especially by combining with oxygen.

paradigm An example showing how something is to be done.

smallpox A sometimes deadly disease that is caused by a virus.

theory A general principle or set of principles that explains facts or events of the natural world.

variable Able to change, or likely to be changed.

FOR MORE INFORMATION

Andronik, Catherine M. *Copernicus: Genius of Modern Astronomy* (Genius Scientists and Their Genius Ideas). Berkeley Heights, NJ: Enslow Publishers, 2015.

Berne, Emma. *Guess! Research and Form a Hypothesis*. New York, NY: PowerKids Press, 2015.

Demuth, Patricia, and John O'Brien. *Who Was Galileo*? New York, NY: Grosset & Dunlap, 2015.

Kneidel, Sally. *Creepy Crawlies and the Scientific Method: More Than 100 Hands-On Science Experiments for Children*. Golden, CO: Fulcrum, 2015.

Lin, Yoming. *Isaac Newton and Gravity*. New York, NY: PowerKids Press, 2012.

Sharkawy, Azza. *Question It!* (Science Sleuths). New York, NY: Crabtree Publishing, 2015.

WEBSITES

The History of Vaccines

https://www.historyofvaccines.org/content/scientific-method

Science Made Simple

http://www.sciencemadesimple.com

SciJinks

https://scijinks.gov/scientific-method
Twitter, Facebook: @SciJinks

INDEX